LEADERSHIP

FOR TURBULENT TIMES

LEADERSHIP
FOR TURBULENT TIMES

Leonard R. Sayles

Center for Creative Leadership
Greensboro, North Carolina

The Center for Creative Leadership is an international, nonprofit educational institution founded in 1970 to advance the understanding, practice, and development of leadership for the benefit of society worldwide. As a part of this mission, it publishes books and reports that aim to contribute to a general process of inquiry and understanding in which ideas related to leadership are raised, exchanged, and evaluated. The ideas presented in its publications are those of the author or authors.

The Center thanks you for supporting its work through the purchase of this volume. If you have comments, suggestions, or questions about any CCL Press publication, please contact the Director of Publications at the address given below.

Center for Creative Leadership
Post Office Box 26300
Greensboro, North Carolina 27438-6300
Telephone 336-288-7210
www.ccl.org/publications

Center for
Creative
Leadership

NORTH AMERICA EUROPE ASIA
www.ccl.org

CCL No. 325

Library of Congress Cataloging-in-Publication Data

Sayles, Leonard R.
     Leadership for turbulent times / Leonard R. Sayles.
          p.   cm.
     Includes bibliographical references.
     ISBN 1-882197-07-0 [ISBN-13: 978-1-882197-07-1]
     1. Leadership. I. Title.
HD57.7.S288 1995
658.4'092—dc20   95-16617
                                                                                  CIP

Table of Contents

Acknowledgment

I would like to thank Meena Wilson for helping to make this report possible. She conducted many of the executive interviews, did much of the analysis of the interview data, and provided critical support and encouragement before and during the conference.

Foreword

In 1994 the Center hosted a conference on "New Demands for Leadership: Responding to Turbulence." A diverse group of participants—including behavioral-science researchers, leadership trainers, corporate executives, and consultants—attempted: to clarify the critical new challenges that executives are facing in these turbulent times; to identify the skills and perspectives executives need to meet these challenges successfully; and to determine the implications for how to select and develop these new skills and perspectives. A number of insights were generated, and since the conference, many Center staff have been able to incorporate these into emerging research and training agendas.

This report is one important conference outcome. It reports on some of the key issues that were raised, and it also represents the personal insights of someone who has devoted a lifetime to observing and thinking about organizations—Len Sayles.

The conference, and this report, would not have been possible without the help of many individuals. The Center gratefully acknowledges the people who attended the conference and made it what it was. Particular thanks and recognition must go to the conference planning committee, including: Bob Burnside, David DeVries, Stan Gryskiewicz, Patti Hall, Martha Hughes-James, Peter Neary, Leonard Sayles, and Meena Wilson. Leonard Sayles served as conference chair, Martha Hughes-James as conference manager, and David DeVries as conference moderator.

Special recognition also must go to the following conference contributors: John S. Bridgeman, British Alcan Aluminum plc; John Cimino, Associated Solo Artists, Inc.; Frank L. Douglas, Marion Merrell Dow Inc.; Cynthia A. Graham, Barnett Card Services Corporation; Ronald A. Heifetz, Harvard University; Madelyn P. Jennings, Gannett Company, Inc.; Thomas W. Jones, TIAA-CREF; Gary E. Jusela, The Boeing Company; Allyn W. Keiser, Canadian Imperial Bank of Commerce; James W. Kuhn, Columbia University; John R. Lauritzen, Jr., AT&T Federal Systems Advanced Technologies; Marcia M. Lefkowitz, Reader's Digest USA; Earle Mauldin, BellSouth Corporation; Edward H. Mertz, General Motors; David M. Noer, Center for Creative Leadership; Ingar Skaug, Wilhelmsen Lines; Lanty L. Smith, Precision Fabrics Group, Inc.; Marilyn Tam, MTA, Inc.; Peter B. Vaill, The George Washington University; Stephen J. Wall, Manus; and Judith Whittaker, Hallmark Cards, Inc.

Walt Tornow
January 1995

Introduction

In recent years the context of business in the United States has undergone a radical change. Following World War II, there was a lengthy period of relative stability when U.S. business was preeminent. Japan and Germany were prostrate, and there were no Southeast Asian tigers. Some economists even presumed that companies could dictate to their customers what they wanted, how much they should purchase, and when (see Galbraith, 1967). For the most part, companies simply sought a greater volume of business, more product flow through a fixed asset base. Quality, service, and cost seemed to take care of themselves. Even poor management was often covered up by inflationary price increases.

Many companies operated in a regulated industry in which the government essentially guaranteed reasonable profitability. This served to further the belief that there were well-defined markets; a finite set of known competitors; relatively fixed, or slowly evolving, technologies; and undemanding customers. As one knowledgeable observer of the post-World War II business world said, "Competition existed more on paper than in practice . . . . There were few sectors of the economy that weren't protected, sheltered, pampered, regulated, or simply rigged" (Chernow, 1994).

Companies assumed that they could predict the future by extrapolating from the past. A small number of senior executives made almost all the important decisions, and those below worked to meet the plan. Middle- and lower-level managers had little discretion and understood that their function was to be a linking pin in a carefully prescribed chain of command (see Likert, 1961). They were rewarded for staying in the box, seeing their own turf in isolation from the rest of the organization, and not questioning the plan.

Almost all change was managed change—carefully spaced improvements to coincide with the planned obsolescence of products and the depreciation of fixed assets.

Employees were often tied to the organization by implicit commitments of long-term employment plus the bonds provided by relatively lucrative pension plans.

Around 1985, however, this extraordinarily benign period ended. Turbulence—or, to use the metaphor introduced by Peter Vaill (1989), permanent white water—became the rule.

The boundary lines between industries began to crumble. It is now almost impossible to define your competitors. Companies must continually redefine their industry focus, transforming themselves, largely as a result of advances in technology.

At the same time the boundaries between organizations are becoming permeable. Vendors are coming in and companies are moving out to their customers. More and more, companies are partnering with former competitors to build joint ventures. Some companies have virtually no central core of assets; almost all of their operations are conducted inside of their partners' organizations.

Customers demand customization, prompt delivery, and price and quality advantages.

There is almost "zero information float." Parity in technology can be reached almost overnight.

Computers make it possible for companies to keep changing methods with little marginal cost.

The employer-employee relationship is in flux (De Meuse & Tornow, 1993), with fear of downsizing an ever-present reality (Noer, 1993a, 1993b). Long-term employment is not guaranteed, and people now expect to live a life of serial employment. Within a given company, employees who work part-time, who work off the premises, and who maintain traditional schedules may work in the same office.

A two-tier workforce seems to be emerging. Many managers in flat, lean organizations are working incredibly long hours, while some employees are seeking less demanding jobs and more leisure for quality time with family and friends.

Profits are continuously threatened by competitive forces. To keep up, companies must introduce, at shorter and shorter intervals, improvements in products and methods; they seek better quality with lower cost.

It is generally recognized that this change in context[1] from stability to turbulence is making new demands on our leaders. At the Center, there has been an ongoing effort to understand these. One of our training programs was specifically designed around the challenges that leaders face in the coming years and the consequent leadership competencies required to take action in response to them (see Burnside & Guthrie, 1992). And in 1994 we convened a working conference on turbulence and the new leadership requirements.

We invited a number of knowledgeable executives to exchange ideas and experiences with leadership researchers from the Center and several universities. Prior to the conference we did extensive interviews with fifteen of the executives to see what they consider the compelling and distinctive challenges of today's business world. There were three major questions that underlaid the interviews: (1) What are the most critical leadership challenges today—the ones that will really make a difference in company performance over time and which are new or different? (2) What is difficult, demanding, or even counterintuitive (or against organizational culture) in coping with these challenges and achieving leadership excellence? (3) What can senior management do to encourage and aid in the development of these leadership capabilities?

From the interview material, we then identified eight themes that captured the forces of change in management: teamwork and organizational stewardship among senior managers; leading beyond the organization's boundaries; rethinking the boss-subordinate, employer-employee relationship; senior executives as exemplars of values; operating excellence—making technology contribute; maintaining strategic focus to grow the business; senior managers who continue to learn; and the impact of U.S. culture on U.S. management.

These themes were used to organize conference activities. Each theme was the subject of a small-group discussion, and participants were assigned to groups according to their expressed interest in the topic. The groups met several times over the course of the conference, observers recorded their insights, and their conclusions were reported back at plenary sessions.

What follows is a personal account of the insights yielded by the conference. For each theme, I first give my impressions on the topic, based on the pre-conference interviews and conference discussions. These are augmented with examples drawn from my own experience, including field work that I did for a CCL-sponsored research project on the leadership demands on middle managers, and examples garnered in my reading of the business press. I then provide a selection of comments by the executives in the interviews and during the conference. These illustrate the evolution in management thinking that has taken place since the demise of the "comfort years." The executive insights are hard-won, often vividly expressed, contradictory, and should help inform future research.

This report, then, is an exploration of the ideas expressed at the conference about the changing context for leadership in U.S. business, the new demands on business leaders, and the skills required to meet those demands.

Teamwork and Organizational Stewardship
Among Senior Managers

One way that organizations have attempted to respond to turbulence is through teamwork,[2] which obviously facilitates the exchange of information, strategy formation, and decision making.

CEOs (and annual reports) often speak glowingly about executive teamwork, but the term often sounds like an oxymoron. Highly competitive, strongly individualistic senior executives can find it difficult to collaborate. One small example: *The Wall Street Journal* (Ingrassia & Mitchell, 1994) claimed that it cost the Ford Motor Company four times as much as it cost Chrysler to develop comparable compact cars for the international market partly because of poor teamwork between Ford's English and German engineering organizations.

The following ideal scenario is drawn from what I have observed in many companies that have been successful in developing cross-functional teamwork at senior levels:

> Senior management in marketing wants the new product to have X feature. Their engineering counterparts argue that to do X would involve very costly and risky new procedures and therefore the new product should not have the X feature. Marketing points out how important X is to consumer acceptance. Engineering, accepting that need, eventually finds a way of building in the X feature at a much lower cost than they originally anticipated.

> Several months later engineering wants to change an existing product feature, Y, because they have discovered a new process for doing some of the product's manufacturing that will (unfortunately) modify Y. Marketing insists that Y can't be changed. When engineering shows that the cost savings will be very substantial, marketing develops a new approach to promoting the product with the modified Y.

When there is good teamwork among executives there can be confrontations and forceful disagreements. These should occur, however, (1) in ways in which relative power and status and concerns with turf are not issues and so that (2) interpersonal, working relationships are not injured. The interplay should presume that relevant knowledge and inputs to the final decision are widely dispersed in the organization and not limited to a particular function or role.

Actually it is somewhat misleading to use the term *executive team* as if it describes a homogeneous category. There are different kinds of executive teams: for instance, executives from diverse functions brought together for a time-bounded project such as designing a new product or marketing campaign; middle managers representing the functions directly impacting customer service—such as sales, logistics, manufacturing, credit and collections, information services—who are assigned to key customers; vendors and customers, so that new designs and components can be optimally and jointly developed; executives from joint-venture partners who come together to facilitate high-cost/high-risk new technology and product-development programs. Each of these probably requires a distinct style of leadership.

It is important to note that these management teams are not like typical worker teams comprised of people who consistently work closely together, develop tight-knit interrelationships, and share common goals and who have little reason to be competitive with one another.

Most managerial teams are organizationally and geographically dispersed and have members who may well be competitive with one another and who don't have that frequency of contact that usually assures good relationships. They are not likely to have identical goals. Thus, the leadership challenges are far greater in these management teams.

Attempts at executive teamwork often flounder because key senior executives have become inflexible barons, maintaining the impregnability of their fiefdoms. Realistically, there are significant differences in the relative organizational power of senior executives. This imbalance often reflects past successes (and career lines), not an assessment of future market and technology realities. Some executives express concern that emerging areas of core competency may lack political power and that these areas could therefore get short-changed on resource allocations.

How can an organization foster the willingness of executives to be responsive to the critical resource needs of peers and the larger organization, to forego credit and even accept some sacrifice? Particularly as the emphasis on effective and timely execution increases, executives who oversee centralized resources face a major challenge in meeting the needs of various operating groups. When they make decisions the needs of external users must carry at least as much weight as internal standards of excellence.

Given these difficulties, new CEOs often feel the need to import intact teams of senior managers with whom they have worked previously and who have a track record of cooperation. Do transplanted executives impede teamwork because they are seen as both different from the local team and much closer to the boss?

Many executives recognize the value of diversity in making better decisions—in experience, functional identification, and style of thinking, as well as in gender and race—but does too much diversity impede cooperation? Executives often seem to think so or there would not be so many relatively homogeneous executive groups.

And where there is real diversity within a management team, the leader has to learn the new and difficult skills of managing multicultural negotiations and how to maintain vigorous, open debate that does not become destructive either to the organization or to individual relationships.

In some cases, too much emphasis on executive teamwork and consensus may drive out important differences of opinion. Executives who have good reason to believe that a particular decision is wrong may be reluctant to speak up if the culture says disagreement is a sign someone isn't a team player. There needs to be a balance between legitimate battles over what is needed to maintain the integrity of a function or division and what should be sacrificed for peers or a larger goal (see Pascale, 1990).

At the conference an important distinction was made between *mavericks* and *rebels*. Neither are good team players. The latter, however, do not have values consistent with the needs of the larger organization. Mavericks, although they are not team-oriented, provide valuable diversity and can be brilliant contributors because they are committed to the organization.

Another useful distinction that was made is the one between *good soldiers* and *conformists*. The latter behave in socially approved, agreeable ways but are not motivated to serve the goals and values of the organization. Good soldiers, on the other hand, are the team players who really seek to advance the interests of the company.

In a similar vein, the insistence on consensus can delay important decisions. Leaders need to know how to balance the contradictory requirements for timely decision making with the needs for solidarity and consensus.

Effective teamwork is distinguished by mutual trust and credibility, an open exchange of information (bad news as well as good), and candor. Yet this type of day-to-day collaboration—where unplanned opportunities and unpredicted problems that require mutual adaptation are identified, where successful experiments in one unit get transplanted to others, and where unforeseen decrements in performance that will impact other divisions are admitted early and addressed vigorously—is rare in senior management.

To function in a highly interdependent organizational and external world, senior executives need multiple perspectives, not parochialism. But they also require in-depth knowledge. How can these be balanced?

They also need a reasonable degree of self-confidence to feel free to exchange ideas and negotiate with peers; however, too much confidence—arrogance—inhibits such exchanges.

How can top management motivate teamwork and assess whether a balance of power and interaction prevails, as well as determine whether mutual accommodation (versus competition) is becoming a norm? How does an executive improve the balance of power within senior-executive teams, particularly when a formerly lower-status function has now moved up to the critical path?

Part of the answer lies in the executive's ability to harmonize divergent interests and personalities and to encourage cooperation in contrast to competition. Aspects of this include devising rewards that balance the more traditional returns for individual achievement. Also, and equally difficult, leaders have to deal decisively with executives who engage in "anti-team" behavior. The test comes when the problems center on executives whose individual performance scores are excellent.

Ultimately, what seems to be needed for executive teamwork to be an effective response to turbulence is for executives to see themselves not as "lone wolf" contributors in pursuit of personal accomplishment but as stewards of their organization working with colleagues towards mutually beneficial goals.

Comments from Executives

"We had close to zero teamwork among senior executives until the survival of the corporation became an issue. Then these top executives began working together. Interestingly, as a result of that experience, they continued to demonstrate some of that teamwork after the crisis was passed."

"CEOs don't have any difficulty spotting teamwork. Some just don't think they need it; their senior people are running independent businesses. Others do need it, but they provide reward systems that aren't compatible with cooperation."

"I don't believe executives should, as they say, stick to their last. They have a critical role to play contributing to other functions. I find it distressing that some of my colleagues impose these restraints on themselves; they don't express opinions about other functions even when they have very relevant knowledge. For example, my head of R&D might have some important ideas about how to increase business with a good customer but would fail to contribute these in the belief that our marketing people would be upset."

"Our lean organization can't afford mistakes like having to do something over. Thus I rely on teamwork to get things coordinated; people have to constantly think in terms of their interdependence with others. My subordinates have to take the time to get outsiders involved and I expect them to negotiate with each other. I further expect them to specify what they need from each other and how they are going to measure how well that is being accomplished."

"Managers unfortunately get very little preparation (in school or at work) in teamwork and collaboration; everything is focused on individual achievement. We also have to learn how to reward those who are good at building teams and those who are good team members."

"In my experience organizations don't give enough recognition (rewards) for teamwork. But the reverse is also true. In some companies there may be too much emphasis on civility, on being polite to the point that people don't say what they think."

"In America everyone looks for the lone wolf; we celebrate them. *Time* magazine doesn't have a team of the year; parents brag about their child, the star. We seek strong leaders, and unlike Japan where several children even play the lead in a school drama, only one child gets the lead part in the U.S."

"Some of our resistance to team play comes from our fear of losing our turn to play the wolf. Some may even reason that they've waited a long time to get a shot at being first and are not happy with all this emphasis on teams now."

"A lot of people believe that teams are just the same as committees—slow and ponderous."

"There is going to be resistance to teams at the functional level in a company when under traditional measures the function shows up as doing very well."

Leading Beyond the Organization's Boundaries

A major aspect of turbulence is the blurring of organizational boundaries. Companies are bringing key vendors "inside"—for instance, to help design new components so that they can be produced with more consistent quality and lower cost. At the same time, they are working inside the walls of other companies—alliance partners and major customers—providing such services as data-base management, project-integration services, or training; they are also collaborating on joint projects. Executives now speak frequently and optimistically about the values of partnering.

In its most extreme form, partnering has led to the development of what is now called the *virtual organization*. A virtual organization retains only a small number of core functions (such as design and finance) and outsources almost everything else. Even functions that once were considered core, such as information-system management, may now be handled by a contractor.

Further complicating this situation, the traditional roles of suppliers, customers, and competitors are in flux. For example, in a recent study of some of IBM's problems (Carroll, 1994), the author concluded that its senior managers failed to develop a stable working relationship with Microsoft. They presumed that Microsoft was in a dependent position as a software provider. Over time, Microsoft shifted roles from being a vendor to being a venture partner, and eventually to becoming a major competitor.

A knowledgeable Silicon Valley executive observed, "In this business everyone is a friend and an enemy—at the same time!" Kodak's new CEO recently noted, "Our competitors and our partners are the same" (Bounds, 1994).

Given this situation, the leadership challenges are numerous. Perhaps the major one is that executives have to change the way they have traditionally acted. In the past, the executive was expected to be a dispassionate judge who would balance the interests of outsiders (customers and suppliers) with those of insiders (employees and shareholders). But now the executive, instead of being an independent decision-maker, must assume the more interactive role of negotiator.

In the past, executives held suppliers at arm's length and the relationship was limited to annual price negotiations. Suppliers were asked to bid on a part or service after the executive had decided all the specifications. Now executives call in vendors very early in the development cycle and people on both sides seek to evolve a design that will be efficient to produce as well as fit a prescribed need.

In doing this, with both alliances and contractors, executives need to be aware of the possibility of exploitation: one party running off with know-how or trade secrets or customers. They must learn to build robust, mutually fruitful relationships of trust and mutually reinforcing collaboration despite these fears and ambiguities.

Leadership is now as much an inter- as an intraorganizational process. Executives have to lead in dealings with vendors, key customers, alliance partners, and community pressure groups (for instance, groups concerned with environmental and racial issues).

The challenge of coordination is increasing. Even in the relatively stable environment of a few years ago, it was very difficult to coordinate the interfaces between adjacent departments in the same company. Now, alliances in high-technology fields require that complex, dynamic interfaces (in software and hardware) be precisely coordinated across multiple organizational boundaries.

Today, many executives have to learn to manage a confederation of semi-autonomous units instead of subordinates (see Byrne, Brandt, & Port, 1993; Hirschorn & Gilmore, 1992). Some observers believe that this confederation arrangement is a new organizational structure (Handy, 1992).

Comments from Executives

"I talked with an executive whose firm was a supplier to a major corporation. They came to him and basically said they were tearing up the only contract they had with them and would expect them to cut their prices very substantially. The executive felt that they might have prevailed if they wanted to fight this abrogation of the contract in court, but it would be a costly process. But in the future, that buyer is going to get an inferior product."

"It takes a lot of training and a good mind to be able to shift from perceiving another executive as the enemy to seeing him or her as friend and collaborator. Most of us were brought up to think of major competitors as the enemy and now we are doing several joint ventures with them. It was easier to motivate people to fight the enemy, but we don't live in that kind of world any longer."

"In our industry, because the customer expects to get what he wants the day he wants it, retailers expect to get what they order within a month. All this requires new interrelationships and new organizational processes involving our sources of supply and our customers—that is, the retailer."

"I watched two CEOs who were courting each other recently considering whether to develop a customer-supplier relationship. It was like they were having a date. Their conversation wasn't directly business (and it wasn't personal or sports). They talked about the future of the computer industry, where it was going and the like. They seemed to want to find out whether the other person was the sort that you would want to have a long-term relationship with."

"In assessing a possible vendor you want to see whether you can really get the commitment of the other people: that they at times will anticipate your needs, go the extra mile, and not simply look at the specifications in the contract."

"The competitors we worry about aren't even in our industry yet."

"Previously our company would give a potential vendor completed designs and get prices and then we would tell the winner to produce it. Now we partner. We get the inputs from the vendor at the same time we are beginning to think through what we will need. Increasingly the vendor adds more services to what he is making in our industry like ticketing, training sales people, doing displays, and even drafting the checks by which he will get paid!"

"We are living the virtual organization. We have almost no fixed assets except our knowledge. We buy everything from outsiders with whom we build close working relations. Even our inventory is owned by others!"

Rethinking the Boss-Subordinate, Employer-Employee Relationship

The relationship between boss and subordinate was once clear-cut, at least in principle if not always in practice. Everyone was in the company for the long run. The boss was cool, rational, even detached. He (or, more rarely, she) delegated as much as possible, keeping hands off the work and motivating subordinates, usually with the promise of future rewards: for instance, promotions, more money. The subordinate, often with more technical knowledge than the boss, because he or she actually did the work, was responsible for fulfilling expectations.

This relationship is changing. There are many reasons why, but one of the more significant ones is that the relationship between the organization and the individual is changing (see De Meuse & Tornow, 1993).

Many companies now have a constantly changing admixture of contract personnel, temporary workers, part-time employees, and employees who have no company workplace but work out of their cars and homes. Oh, yes, there are also full-time, "official" regular employees!

Historically, the company supplied job security, attractive benefits such as pensions and medical plans, and promotions; in return, employees concentrated on their jobs and gave the company their complete loyalty. Now, job security is often in doubt, particularly as downsizing becomes more common;

benefits are being cut; and promotions in smaller, flatter organizations are much less likely.

Consider the following example of the diminishment of job security: At Connecticut Mutual Life Insurance, top management has decided that every position in the company should be considered a new job. Thus, existing employees will have to reapply for their old jobs and be evaluated relative to the skills that a new employee would bring to that job. Their management believes there is value in creating deliberate chaos. The CEO describes the strategy this way: "What we're introducing is uncertainty in an organization that has for 140 years worked on getting rid of every shred of uncertainty. . . . I want there to be the right amount of anxiety in the system" (Johnson, 1994).

A much larger company, Avon Products, adopted a similar stance in its marketing department: "All executives . . . were forced to reapply for redesigned jobs; a third failed to get the new positions" (Hwang, 1994). This is surely an extreme strategy, but it underlines the shift that is taking place between managements that placed a high value on providing job security and the new downsizing era.[3]

At the same time, demands on managers keep increasing: Leaner organizations, greater frequency of change, tougher coordination problems all show up as tougher jobs and work loads. In some companies the combination of part-timers and full-timers gives the manager a much larger group to supervise. Some executives are now handling three or four jobs that were once handled by separate managers.

Yet it is not uncommon now for executives to question how much of themselves they should give at the office. Many reject transfers even when they involve significant promotions. Some are interested in earning less, having more quality time with their families, not working the sixty-to-eighty-hour weeks required by typical tough managerial jobs.

Faced with all this, we must rethink our understanding of the relationship between boss and subordinate and between employer and employee. This, in turn, will require us to develop a new understanding of leadership requirements and leadership development practices. Let me give some examples.

In our studies at CCL (Sayles, 1993, p. 253) there is data suggesting that managers, particularly in situations where change is frequent, often need to get involved in the details of work in order to understand the issues confronting subordinates and to provide direct assistance in solving problems interfering with effective performance. This is because most work is not programmed to stay integrated throughout work systems and produce high performance (Sayles, 1990). Leaders will have balance delegation and autonomy with the ability to intervene and take over at certain times.

Acquiring the technical knowledge that enables executives to do this effectively in organizations with dynamic markets and technologies probably requires at least three or four years in place. In the past, many organizations have sought to develop executives by moving high-potentials every year or two. This may be counterproductive.

In fast-moving companies, good subordinates may need to be assertive (both with bosses and peers) and sometimes assume responsibilities greater than their delegated authority. Highly educated, motivated employees may have special leadership needs.

The detachment fostered by the former boss-subordinate relationship is probably no longer a good leadership strategy. We have data suggesting that high motivation is the result of working for a high-performance organization rather than high motivation being the cause of improved performance. And subordinates usually respond positively to the personal involvement and passion of their bosses for the goal and vision of the business; they are not necessarily distressed by the occasional emotional outburst of the really involved boss. Further, it is at least plausible that truly committed executives show more emotion because they are more dedicated to improving their organizations.

A fundamental task for managers today is to provide continuing challenge and reinforcement to high-performing subordinates—now that there are few binding organizational ties (see Kelley, 1988; Peace, 1991).

Comments from Executives

"I observe that there are really two quite different kinds of CEOs. There are those who are well adjusted, not neurotic, and who genuinely care for people. Then there are those who I would call almost idiot savants. They display paranoid tendencies, but they're brilliant when it comes to running a business. They are truly a lot smarter than most other people they encounter. They're often great at running an organization undergoing a crisis. But you can't expect them to be very good with people."

"I want my subordinates to feel as free to disagree with my ideas as they would with a peer."

"In my organization we've been through one reorganization after another for twenty years; people need some stability."

"I often cross-examine subordinates very vigorously; they may not understand that I am checking how they will stand up under that kind of pressure. Also I need to assure myself if I am going to be a vigorous advocate for them. People in senior management have limited technical knowledge so they will be seeing how well people respond to this cross-examination process, how well prepared they are."

"I never give orders. And there is no reason to act powerfully like a boss either; everyone knows I'm the boss. Thus I spend my time inspiring, motivating, persuading, and questioning my people. In fact I have to be careful that things I say aren't interpreted as orders. I might mumble something about not liking the color of one of my walls and the next day it would be repainted."

"With greater empowerment, the boss's emphasis needs to be much more on balancing multiple interests and dealing with ambiguous, contradictory data and requests. I am suspicious of a subordinate who waits for orders; I expect them to take initiative."

"It's not, 'We will take care of you' any more; it's, 'You take care of yourself.' And management ranks are being stripped to flatten organizations, so the dangling carrot—an opportunity for promotion—is not as ready an incentive. Some younger employees seem less dedicated to the need to be economically self-sufficient and are therefore less serious about a job, working hard, and not living off Mom and Dad."

"I see successful leaders primarily as 'pushy colleagues' and network builders. Also, they are good at self-disclosure of their vulnerabilities."

"The new generation of subordinates can be very puzzling, particularly to older executives. I have a superb technical person who wants to work part-time; another wants to work in his office at home much of the time (so he can work all hours and not be disturbed). We also have people who want to get extra time off to be with their children and many are much more interested in nonwork (family, leisure) than work."

"We now have what I call the *Vietnam-generation employee*. I never thought there was any alternative to working twelve-hour days."

"Some of the people we've identified as high-potentials, who twenty years ago would have said when asked to move from Dallas to New York, 'Yes, sir,' now say, 'No way; it's not worth it and I am not going. Yes, I know it may hurt my career, but my wife is making $75,000 and I'm making $120,000. We're doing fine and I don't need to improve my chances.'"

"I've heard several times recently when new managerial recruits are surveyed as to what is important to them, security and balanced lifestyle comes before opportunities for advancement and compensation."

"We need managers who will put in seventy-to-eighty-hour weeks! Very many are unwilling to do this regardless of rewards. In fact, many are looking to take less pay for more leisure."

"There are so many uncertainties today that it is hard to plan the development of people. In the old days we could hire someone with the right technical background and put them into the proper sequence of jobs and know that in fifteen years, say, you would have a specific kind of product manager. No more."

"We want people who will be responsible for their own careers. We preach that employees have to take care of themselves. We will help them to develop their skills and try to make the best use of them. Also, we would like to link pay to skill development. But since what is going to happen in the company tomorrow is uncertain, it is sensible for employees to develop a marketable personal professionalism. We know the danger in that is that unless we use people properly they will jump ship."

"I think most upper-middle managers stopped some time ago thinking of the company as some sacrosanct entity that was going to be loyal to them. They had seen too many mergers. They recognize that there is no "they" running the company; the "they" is in flux and no one really gives a damn about long-term employment. Most of these people rewrote their contracts dealing with loyalty a long time ago."

"A really good leader can get her own people to make suggestions about redundancies and waste in their department even when some jobs may be at risk. Unfortunately our management-appraisal and reward systems don't identify these leaders."

"To be accepted as a leader, you need to be willing to talk about things you did wrong and even a little about your personal life."

"You need to set personal standards in how hard you work. You can't come in at nine and leave at five and expect your subordinates are going to really commit to their jobs."

"You not only have to set the vision and get people excited about that vision but you have to demonstrate that you are there with your people every step of the way. The visibility of the leader is vitally important because you are seeking to motivate people to uproot their traditional views (of their jobs and how things are done). Your job is to be out in front with a flag waving. You can't ever let people think there is something more important in your field of vision. But this is a tough balancing act; there will be other things you have to do (separate from fulfilling the vision you have given). These need to be fitted in with the need to appear to be there all the time for your people.

From a subordinate to their manager: "You are going to be hard to replace. Most managers around here are not 'fighters.' You have absolutely devoted yourself to fighting for us and for your vision of the kind of department we should be and the needs of our customers. And that personal courage is going to be hard to find."

"In a lean organization like ours, every manager now has four jobs!"

"I have been distressed to find that it is some of our younger managers who are most resistant to creating a fast-paced organization. Many Harvard MBAs talk about the importance of a vision but what they really think about is their own compensation. They are obsessed with titles and the amount of power they have, even the size of their offices and the number of people they manage. Now we don't equate titles or status to numbers of people managed and we all have small offices."

"I have never been in an organization where the organization (not me) hasn't 'fired' a person before I have to."

"I want diversity in my workforce primarily to get a mix of ideas. It concerns me when everyone sees things the same way when we first begin exploring an issue or a decision."

"You need to work at creating a system that will bring up the bad news; you don't have to worry about good news. It will find you."

"Those who work for you are more likely to really contribute to the organization's performance when they believe they can make a difference. You get major contributions from those who feel they are the proprietor of a business—that is, they have a sense of ownership."

Senior Executives as Exemplars of Values

In the midst of turbulence, people naturally seek a stable lodestar. The most obvious are the enduring values of an organization. How do executives shape the values of subordinates? Historically, research has shown that leaders can affect followers by demonstrating personal integrity (for instance, their word is their bond, they "walk their talk") and their personal commitment to core organizational values. Thus, leaders can be a stabilizing influence by giving of themselves to represent subordinates, taking care to develop their people, and making personal sacrifices.

Unfortunately, there may be an increasing self-centeredness on the part of executives. Too frequently the desire to score high and win has caused executives to let standards slip and even violate the law. They can also undercut values when they drive subordinates into unethical behavior by placing undue pressure on them for results. With extraordinary regularity, the press carries stories about executives who lie and cheat with respect to performance measures. Although some of these events represent the actions of what appear to be amoral individuals, most represent the reaction to extraordinarily harsh pressures from superiors for good results at any cost. It is often made clear to subordinates that they must somehow find a way to make the numbers for the previous fiscal period look good or else.

Many facets of the senior manager's world may encourage this self-centeredness. Some executives reason that, after all, they are the winners in a hotly contested struggle to get to the top and deserve an easier life and very high compensation and special perks. The enormous personal gains associated with bonus and option plans, a kind of winner-take-all mentality, can cause some managers to forget their responsibilities to subordinates and to destroy what little confidence may remain in the value of organizational loyalty.[4]

Thus, the issue of the need for senior leaders to restrain their pursuit of winning, of personal goals, pay, and benefits seems particularly important in this turbulent age.

In a business world in which long-standing implicit employment contracts have had to be abrogated and job insecurities are many, how do leaders symbolize their commitment to a fundamental and generally shared position that we refer to as *human values*? Many of us believe that a situation in which managers compete with each other to determine who receives the highest return—values that seem to dominate Wall Street firms—does not serve organizations well. It would be more organizationally effective to have interpersonal as well as intergroup cooperation and a commitment to the needs of the total organization. How difficult is it to identify early those executives with overriding needs for self-seeking?

How does a leader demonstrate personal integrity? What are the guideposts for deciding how to balance and make trade-offs among personal, organizational, and subordinate needs and goals? How difficult is it to distinguish: (a) between aggressive managers who primarily serve the organization versus aggressive managers who callously abuse others and primarily serve themselves; (b) between those who are politically sophisticated (realistic) versus those whose success comes from their political, not work, skills; and (c) between those who are flexible and adaptive versus those who shift positions whenever they sense opposition or learn which way the political wind is blowing?

Senior executives need to exemplify by their personal behavior and day-to-day involvement: the organization's core values, acceptance of reasonable risk, and the willingness to hear bad news. Thus, they need to spend some of their time on whatever are the front lines of the business. But is this realistic, given the increased needs for external involvements and the temptation to move away from the dreary, demanding, and complex problems of the business when one has been promoted to the very senior levels of the company?

More companies are talking about identifying and supporting their core values. But how does a leader exemplify an organization's core values? And how does that leader build a consensus around those values?

Here is how Hewlett-Packard's founders and senior executives impart some critical values (Deutchman, 1994, p. 90):

> H-P's vigor comes in large part from the management philosophy and values imparted over five decades by the pair [William Hewlett and David Packard] who though retired, still keep watch over the place. A lasting symbol of their frugality and fiscal conservatism . . . can be found at the main R&D complex. But Bill and Dave (as they are known to all) refuse to allow any changes in their offices . . . tacky shag carpeting . . . plain inexpensive wood paneling. . . . It's [also] considered bad form at H-P to trumpet one's personal achievements.

> Senior managers typically joined when fresh out of engineering school in . . . unglamorous, but hands-on jobs. Almost all have spent their entire career at H-P . . . and are likely to have earned their degrees at middlebrow [colleges].

> H-P executives have an enviable degree of freedom . . . the authority to reinvest the capital their businesses generate. They can attack markets in their own ways, rather than slavishly wait for orders that reduce them to just one part of a corporate strategy.

Here we see modelled the values of frugality; care with corporate assets as if they were one's own; modesty; personal responsibility and initiative; and the importance of personal, hands-on work experience for executives.

It is interesting to observe how two U.S. companies with similar values made opposite decisions about doing business in China. Reebok decided to continue to use factories there and in Southeast Asia as long as these contractors paid "appropriate wages in the light of national practices," maintained safe working conditions, and did not use child labor. In contrast, Levi Strauss stopped using Chinese contractors on the grounds that it would not do work in countries where there were pervasive violations of basic human rights (Cox, 1994).

Business requires that very difficult trade-offs be made: for instance, between the resource needs of currently profitable services and investments in innovations that will produce future profits, between concerns for people and the bottom line, between delegation and hands-on managing, and between respect for rules and improvisation. These trade-offs, as we see in the cases of Reebok and Levi Strauss above, also involve judgment and interpretation.

In managing these trade-offs, however, there must be values that encourage the avoidance of simply seeking to maximize the most quantitative or most visible kind of performance.

Comments from Executives

"As a consultant I find that one of the paradoxes in trying to assess what it takes to be a successful senior executive is this contradiction: There are CEOs who really genuinely care for their people and who aren't neurotic, self-destructive, or destructive of others. On the other hand there are also very bright, successful CEOs who are destructive, even paranoid. Many are brilliant, although they can be like idiot savants, narrowly brilliant and insensitive to anything but their specialty. They have such an enormous sense of purpose and ability to separate everything else out of their life but winning that they are particularly useful in crises . . . of which we have more and more in business today. And once they have 'rescued' the company they often stay on."

"Most people in fact want to see their organizations follow the same values that they learned in Sunday school."

Operating Excellence—Making Technology Contribute

During the relatively stable period that followed the Second World War, executives did not pay much attention to operations. Instead, they tended to focus on elaborate business plans. Finding the right product and high volume was their goal.

The turbulence of the past few years, however, has meant that work could no longer be allowed to take care of itself. For one thing, products and services have to revised much more quickly; work systems must thus be repeatedly altered. For another, competition is much keener; therefore, profits come not from one or two right management decisions but from continuous improvement in day-to-day performance (doing things better, making marginal changes).

The radical shift in emphasis from planning to operations has been described by a variety of popular slogans: *high-performance organizations, lean manufacturing, total quality management,* or, more recently, *reengineering.* But what is often ignored is that these all have a common core: the emphasis on the integration and coordination of functions and tasks around work flow.[5]

Thus far, little attention has been devoted to the leadership consequences of the new requirements for managers to excel at managing work (but see Brandt, 1994; Sayles, 1993). Many leadership models seem to assume that work systems can be designed perfectly and only subordinate ineptness or lack of motivation create problems. In fact, as systems become more complex—for instance, as there are more interdependencies within and between organizations—numerous, unpredictable glitches occur, and complex, modern technologies are unstable systems—that is, very small problems can create major disasters.

When managers have their hands off and cannot initiate work-flow improvements, problems fester or employees get blamed or both. Employees themselves can become critical of and demoralized by superiors who are poor at improving performance. "The chairman of USAir's pilot's union was pleased when the carrier named a new chief operating officer. . . . 'USAir [in the past] wasted opportunities to schedule them [pilots] more often and expand flight operations'" (McCarthy, 1994).

Ultimately, keeping hands off can have disastrous effects. Some years ago, a premier U.S. company used its expertise in technology to develop an important component for consumer color television sets. The product became very profitable, and the company was probably the largest supplier of that component. However, the company did not continue to invest in process improvements, and gradually it both lost market share and saw its profits erode as competitors had lower costs. Given its poor margins, senior management did not approve additional investments in operations that would have lowered cost—and improved manufacturing quality. This downward spiral was eventually halted when management realized that it would either have to improve operations or give up that business.

What can we say about the kind of leadership required by the emphasis on operations and work? First, solving unanticipatable problems and fine-tuning, in real time, depend upon the actions of high-initiative, involved managers who are willing to take much more responsibility than in the past. Second, managers will have to be very familiar with work systems, markets, and technologies (see Sayles, 1993).

In order to get this knowledge, managers will have to stay more closely in touch with customers and markets. Many of the decisions formerly made by strong staff and technical groups will have to be made or, at least, shaped by the manager in order to make these technical decisions fit the work-flow requirement. (Many knowledgeable observers believe that little of the potential of the computer revolution is realized because users are so dependent on staff or vendor "techies" with different goals and perspectives.)

The managers who achieve operating excellence will have to be willing to process vast quantities of information almost daily to stay abreast and to identify nascent problems before they become costly. It is a tough challenge to balance, on the one hand, providing subordinates with a sense of autonomy and, on the other, asserting the manager's need to have intimate information about the work and actual involvement in some of the subordinate's decision making. If managed well, the downside of additional involvement is more than balanced by the leader's ability to aid subordinates by persuading external groups to institute changes that resolve internal sources of work frustration.

The perfecting of operations probably requires a newly promoted executive to take several years to gain an in-depth knowledge of, and a real feel for, the work systems, people, and embedded problems and to implement solutions. This conflicts with the expectation that a successful manager should be promoted every year or two and with some current rotational practices in management development programs.

Also, the use of incentives, based on hitting quantitative targets, may injure overall performance. They are often a poor substitute for good leadership, even a crutch for inept managers. Given the complexity of the leader's role, it seems a contradiction to measure its effectiveness by a single number (and to presume that measuring results quantitatively can substitute for knowing your people and the work). Certainly, clear targets can be useful, but how can targets be used without their being destructive?

In many companies, job-evaluation plans are heavily weighted, at middle levels of the organization, in favor of formal education and technical training. Thus, it is not unusual to see staff executives getting significantly more salary than line managers. The former may work a nine-to-five day, with little stress or pressure for performance, while the line executive works seven to seven and under constant pressure. Are there ways of compensating managers adequately for the ever-increasing work loads associated with fast-changing, lean organizations seeking to attain and maintain world-class competitiveness?

Leaders who are successful in creating seamless integration, quick customer responsiveness, and high-quality performance have to make many tough trade-offs among demands from upper management, peers, and their own internal systems integrity. The skills required to deal with these contradictions and inconsistencies and to challenge both bosses and peers are often ignored in discussions of good leadership. Relevant here as well are the leadership skills of balancing hierarchical demands, the standards of staff groups, and the leader's own unit needs of systems integrity.

What is perhaps most demanding and least appreciated about leadership for operating excellence is the extent to which effective managers have to be willing to invest efforts and take organizational risks that are far greater than their likely rewards.

Many companies have announced that they will outsource some critical support functions, such as their information services, to cut costs. To the extent that there is a need for continuing dialogue and quick responsiveness (as between key operating groups and a technical support area), creating a new external relationship could conflict with the renewed emphasis on operating excellence.

Comments from Executives

"How can line managers coordinate innovation when the technology is changing so rapidly that you can't see the new directions until it's too late? And how can senior management encourage and support constant attention to process improvements, doing more with less, because good enough today will not be good enough tomorrow?"

"Advancing technologies need capital investment. But vested interest in elegant new technologies can divert attention from the real goal, which is not to become technologically literate but to maximize the added value the business can deliver. It is backwards to buy technology and try and make it work in the business, rather than design work process and get the technology that supports it."

"There is a strong possibility that a major drug company which had serious quality problems with the manufacture of some of its ethical drugs (including publicly embarrassing disciplining by the FDA) had made a serious error when it created a separate P&L for manufacturing and rewarded those executives on the basis of their profitability."

"Executives need an in-depth knowledge of one functional field so that they realize how much one needs to know about that field or area in order to make sensible choices (and that it can't be learned in a brief period or understood solely in broad brush strokes). They also need to know how and be willing to invest in building a network that covers the system within which they are working. And then they need to know how to get inside the thought boxes of those people who are impacting them and whom they are impacting."

"Executives should have status and compensation commensurate with how much value they add, not how far they have climbed the hierarchy."

"You have to motivate people to go after every opportunity to do things more effectively in this new world. No longer can you have costs any higher than your best competitor and survive."

"I once saw this framed on a CEO's desk: 'To be successful you need to remember that there is no limit to what you can accomplish if you don't care who gets the credit.'"

"Effective executives are comfortable both with ambiguity and working outside what I call their *comfort zone*."

"In the past, most managers were good at passing information down and reports up and making sure no one made a mistake; that's all."

"MBAs got all their training in how to think like a CEO, not on the micro-skills of execution. They took those for granted; they were someone else's problem."

"Motivation comes in part from people being proud of their product."

"Increasingly we have technologies which allow us to do things in a very different way with almost zero marginal cost (given the power of computers) but we need effective managers who can exploit this potential. Thus, for me, the good managers are those who keep pushing the envelope and are able to work out of the box."

"We say that an executive in charge of a critical centralized resource has to coordinate with operating groups. But *coordinate* is a weasel word. What does it mean? Executives in charge of centralized functions or services need to make real-time and innovative trade-offs (in terms of how they respond to demands for service from other units of the corporation) that are different from what has been done historically or that is specified in some manual. And those trade-offs have to be consistent with the trade-offs the line operating managers are making in their dealings with outside customers."

Maintaining Strategic Focus to Grow the Business

It is especially difficult to stay focused in a turbulent environment. Most successful companies, however, owe a significant share of their growth to the ability of senior management to support a strategy over a long period of time. For instance, Motorola grew as a result of its top management's adherence to the strategy that the company should be the world leader in developing technology to be used for "communication with people and machines on the move."

There are usually many tempting distractions, such as acquisition possibilities, that seem easier and more exciting than championing and aiding the painful development of a complex new product or service—with the inevitable frustrations inherent in the vicissitudes of new-product development, unanticipated costs—all threatening profit goals and Wall Street's favor.

It is not easy to stay the course, but when it is done, strategic focus can provide a sense of vital purpose, a cause that continuously challenges good people to give their best, as well as providing the clarity of direction necessary for subordinates to make tough choices among competing interests.

In a sense, a basic responsibility of very senior executives is the development of the organization's capacity and competence to accomplish a certain set of objectives, to function effectively in certain markets or with certain technologies.

Many dilemmas are embedded in this leadership requirement: for instance, the high risk of uncertain future markets and technologies, required trade-offs of time and attention. Efforts to develop the business must be openly and personally protected and nurtured, a difficult choice in a world of fast-changing markets and technology and an uncertain future.

Often, because self-confidence is a requirement for leadership, many CEOs have difficulty distinguishing their own ego needs and self-gratification from serving the long-run interests of the organization. The two become inextricably intertwined (Kegan, 1982). A typical example is what is cynically called the CEO's "edifice complex"—that is, the tendency for a CEO to want to put up a building that will become a lasting reminder of his or her tenure. Also, it is often difficult to distinguish between blind, stubborn persistence and courageous staying of the course.

Because success and failure are observable, and failure can be very costly, leaders put their reputations on the line. It is useful to ask what leadership requirements are embedded here and are they the ones that can be identified in lower-level managerial jobs? Under what circumstances are those with these skills likely to be pushed off the faster track?

And, as is true of almost all other aspects of management, leaders have to juggle their pursuit of key strategic goals with many other legitimate concerns and pressures. Most troubling, the tenure of CEOs is often shorter than the time required to prove out the market reaction of a major innovation. What are the implications of this for leadership?

New strategies often require that previously neglected or poorly developed functions and capabilities gain greater recognition, more resources, and more competent executives. Over time, what were considered less important functions probably retained only mediocre managers, which in turn confirmed the lesser importance of the function. For instance, new CEOs often find that the organization's fine technology-development skills are wasted because of the absence of effective marketing. How does an executive quickly reverse the spiral inherent in this situation? In raising the status and visibility of one function, do others get threatened?

It is likely that middle managers who are most successful will become more entrepreneurial, looking for new outlets (both within the firm and outside) to exploit and leverage their hard-won operating-performance competencies. These important efforts can become what have been called *autonomous strategic initiatives*, strategy that grows out of the capabilities and experience of middle-level managers (see Burgelman, 1983). Thus, strategy-making is not solely the province of top management.

Traditionally, strategy-makers were expected to distance themselves from everyday business. Management researchers now emphasize how good strategies are often emergent. Thus, the strategy-maker needs to be immersed in some of the everyday technology-market issues (Mintzberg, 1987). As such they are seeking to extract larger meaning from the day-to-day routines.

Thus, evolving and maintaining a strategic focus closely relates to the executive as learner (see next section). This shifts executives further from the older models of the isolated decision-maker engaged in rational thinking. It suggests that executives need to act in order to think, just as they also think before acting.

Executives are shifting dramatically the foundation of their strategies. Until recently strategies were built on an enemy model: besting the competition. Managers now often focus on satisfying the customer, a more challenging criterion than succumbing to the lure of traditional war games.

Inherent in maintaining a strategic focus are three special leadership abilities: vision, decisiveness, and sensible risk-taking. How can these be operationalized so that they can be assessed and recognized and developed in our senior management cadres?

Here's one example: Vision appears to relate to an individual's ability to master and then internalize and integrate an enormously broad range of technical, social, and economic factors—in contrast to having a narrow focus, say, on some functional skill. On the face of it we would have to assume this is a rare capability.

Unfortunately, terms such as *vision* often become mantras; everyone speaks well of it but, like *charisma*, it is not well assessed and becomes easy to fake. And, similarly, it can be difficult to distinguish willfulness or arrogance from decisiveness, and foolhardiness from sensible risk-taking.

How can senior executives become more artful in asking questions that will enable them to gather the kind of intelligence useful in both strategy formulation and implementation as well as assess the technical competence of those providing the answers?

Comments from Executives

"The very successful new CEOs that one reads about have a basic skill. When they come in they say these things aren't working and we're wasting our money pouring money into them. We'll get rid of them. These others are our strengths and we concentrate there."

"I have come to believe that most successful strategies are emergent. Nobody is really smarter than the times they live in. To be sure some people have a vision and it just happens to coincide with what happens. The other kind of strategy is very common these days. Things are going badly in a particular company; it is likely to be in a crisis and so they turn to someone who appears to be good at getting the company through the crisis. That is really their strategy, but they will stay on top after the crisis."

"To me the critical skill is picking your values, knowing what it is you want to accomplish. Then the executive chooses issues to address that help further their agenda."

"Strategy-making is a tough balancing act, because there is always another constituency that has to be served. When the pressures for profit grow, how do you take the long-term view that will grow the business? Timeliness is important, for if you string out change, its full force is lessened, other things take a dominant role, and you never get the change."

"There is often an absence of clear strategic thinking. Many managers don't think about their businesses in a generic way, about the need to sow the seeds for the businesses that are going to make the big money in 2025. Marketplace competition makes it critical to learn how to balance strategic effectiveness with operating efficiency."

"Successful executives are able to maintain a broad overview, like the view of a forest from an airplane, with the ability to see each individual tree, all the fine detail."

"Too many executives have trouble dealing simultaneously with all the new external factors that are impacting the company's strategy, or likely to, and still being able to handle the administrative chores and interpersonal issues."

"Most employees need a simple message conveying the strategy and the vision. A good manager is one who can take complexity and reduce it to a simple (not simplistic) message that is easy to comprehend."

Senior Managers Who Continue to Learn

We hear a lot today about developing the learning organization. Chrysler, for example, has recently named a vice president to manage a process in which the company would continuously challenge existing ways of doing things (Simison, Lavin, & Mitchell, 1994). What we don't hear nearly as much about is the necessity for individual executives to continue learning.

Research conducted by the Center (Bunker & Webb, 1992) and my own field data suggest that leaders find it very difficult to depart from what have been winning strategies, except perhaps in a survival crisis. Even then, as pressures and stress increase, there can be a tendency to rely on established modes of behavior and to ignore data that suggest that behavior is ineffective.

More than thirty years ago a series of well-publicized research studies demonstrated that the critical problems of business were less hierarchical control than coordination among functions. Now, reengineering has become one of management's hot buttons—long after high costs, long cycle times, and internal squabbling helped drive business offshore. Why should it have taken thirty years to get management interested in systems, flat organizations, and operating effectiveness?

Several years ago, in interviewing returned expatriates in U.S. multinationals, I was surprised at one consistent theme. The executives were distressed that their colleagues had no interest in finding out what they had learned in their overseas assignments. Even when a replacement was to be sent overseas to the same country, it was rare for the returned executive to be debriefed. No one wanted to learn from their experience!

The recent conglomerate movement also illustrates management's—in this case, senior management's—disdain for learning. Surely those executives who bundled together so many unrelated companies must have believed that they did not have to learn anything about the industries, markets, or technologies they were entering as long as they were in a position to oversee the numbers. In a similar vein, the rapid movement of talented executives from function to function presumes that there is little in-depth learning required.

We know that unlearning, giving up beliefs and patterns of behavior that had been rewarding in the past, can be most difficult. Products, functions, and strategies that were once winners usually continue to dominate decision making, and newcomers have a difficult time getting resources or even air time at critical management meetings (see Miller, 1990).

Dated analogies and metaphors persist and interfere with a realistic understanding of current business challenges. For instance, sports and the military are still the most popular metaphors used by executives. But, as Professor James Kuhn wrote me before the conference, "Business is neither a sport—with a clear winner and loser and with carefully defined rules and an impartial umpire—nor a military operation—very hierarchical, with subordinates having strong patriotic motives to defeat the enemy at any personal cost."

We do hear executives speak more today about a teaching role being central to leadership, but it is interesting that the reference is usually to teaching the organizational ropes. There is little reference to helping subordinates become more proficient technically, to assisting them in learning the dynamics of the work systems that they must interact with and new paradigms about markets and technology. To do this well, managers probably have to be good practitioners as well as teachers, meaning they have to be involved in operations, the basic work of the organization.

Managers often speak openly of the continued practice of shooting the messenger who brings bad news. The result of this practice is well known: Executives, at least at higher levels, are insulated from reality. Without continuous feedback, particularly about negatives—what isn't working that we thought would be so successful—learning is handicapped. Without a feedback loop there is no learning.

Another impediment to executive learning is excessive specialization— a well-known characteristic of U.S. business. For example, almost every large U.S. corporation has a diversity program that in part deals with communication problems among people of different nationalities, gender, or race. But what about communication problems deriving from the interrelationships of functional groups, such as marketing and R&D, that appear to speak totally different languages and distrust each other (Burgelman & Sayles, 1986)? And what about problems deriving from managers crossing corporate or national borders? These are also diversity issues, but they are dealt with as another specialty.

In the past, excessive use of specialized staff inhibited executive learning. Traditionally, managers often turned new or difficult problems over to staff rather than seek to expand their own knowledge; and staff executives, eager to maintain or expand their franchise, have not encouraged the users of their services to become more technically literate and proficient. Efforts to make the organization leaner might reduce such inhibitions.

Similarly, learning about organizational systems and what shapes performance is impeded by the practice of hiring consultants for almost every new technical issue that arises. The manager's own knowledge base does not expand, and he or she is dependent on the consultant. Executives might learn from consultants if the latter were chosen on the basis of their ability to increase the proficiency of the users of their information rather than solely on their ability to propose good solutions to problems.

How have executives managed to avoid learning in the face of so much evidence that things weren't working? For one thing, they seem to have had a love affair with new programs and one-shot fix-its (and adding new specialists). Each solution seems pragmatic, maybe even a panacea. For example, in the past decade executives have layered on, one after the other, in many companies: *just-in-time, kaizen, lean, high performance, Japanese, total quality management*, and now *reengineering, business-process redesign*, and *horizontal organizations*. Every day you read about another senior executive discovering the current management infatuation—cross-functional teams. (Yes, they are useful, very useful, but better companies have known this for decades!)

Companies wasted large sums bringing in one new program after another rather than rethinking their basic premises surrounding the organization of work. But one of the more critical components in learning is the ability to understand one's current framework, belief system, theories, models—whatever you want to call it.

Most executives, however, aren't comfortable with looking for the underlying theories or models from which their decisions flow. They are impatient when discussions turn to basic concepts. This may well reflect their pride in being hard-headed realists and their deep-seated belief that theory is bad.

This aspect of the learning challenge relates to the well-known propensity of executives for short answers: one-page executive summaries, briefing papers, and cover letters. As one experienced consultant said, "Most executives don't want to know why, just what." Thus, concepts and theory are ignored in favor of crisp answers. This is consistent with a distinctly American cultural value: Be pragmatic; theory is soft stuff, only for academics (and students).

This propensity allows new jargon and repackaging to disguise the underlying similarities (and conceptual underpinnings) of various improvement programs. It would appear that although technology transfer is generally given lots of attention in multinationals, it is largely ignored with respect to management principles and techniques.

Underlying the continued emphasis on buying the newest fad and embedding it in a company-wide program or undertaking frequent major, disruptive reorganizations is the management belief that there is one best way of doing things.

Yet another impediment to learning is the well-recognized distaste that many managers have for ambiguity (and contradiction). Managers like clarity and consistency. Regrettably these characteristics are increasingly scarce in a turbulent world.

Organizational skunk works, as they have been called, have been conceived of as learning centers because they are, in a sense, off-line. Because learning is impeded in the predominant culture where most thinking and acting is part of a tightly interlocked, self-reinforcing system, isolated, buffered free-idea zones can be a mechanism for generating new knowledge.

Many managers at least pay lip service to the value of experimentation. But they can be slow in adopting innovations developed by a distant operation or skunk works. For example, General Motors is just now beginning to get buy-in from other divisions for the innovations in selling pioneered years ago by their Saturn Division.

Still another barrier to learning is what an executive at the conference called "the mask of competency." As this term suggests, many executives are afraid to admit, even to themselves, that they don't know something. Such apparent omniscience is surely inconsistent with the posture of one seeking to learn. It bars productive interchanges with subordinates. It also impedes learning from peers, and probably is a major bar to the kind of team interchanges that produce good answers to problems where there is conflict.

Executives who feel they can and do learn often extol the virtues of what could be called a *learning network*: an organizationally dispersed set of well-maintained personal relationships. This diversity in expertise can facilitate the manager's technical and managerial learning. But the network requires managers to invest time in building easy give-and-take relationships with unfamiliar people who are not part of the chain of command. The other requirement appears to be that managers have to learn how to both judge trustworthiness and be perceived as trustworthy and having integrity.

It is not surprising that corporate boards of directors assume they have to change top management to reflect new problems and opportunities; the senior managers in place will usually not be able to learn to act differently.

It can be very costly to dispose of the old and bring in new management. There is good evidence that dynamic, complex technologies require continuity in managerial ranks; and a good deal of organizational learning (know-how, relationships, tacit knowledge) gets lost with turnover.

Executives must transform themselves. Change requires leaders who truly understand the underlying new conceptual issues and can then patiently rework the organization's culture to facilitate organizational learning.

Executives must also force themselves to have more diverse and contentious subordinates and encourage more open competition among ideas and viewpoints. Good leadership thus seems to require the continuous rebalancing of inconsistent, competing values.

I believe that the most important new learning is that there needs to be a constant internal (in the mind of the executive) struggle against psychologically comfortable formula answers, managing on autopilot, managing based on past successes.

Finally, executives must learn how to learn. That is, they must learn to see what is actually taking place in relation to customers, competitors, and internal systems. As stated by the nineteenth-century French writer, Charles Peguy, "Above all, which is very difficult, one must always see what one sees." The last is a proper response to the old Yogi Berra quotation, "You can observe a lot just by watching."

Comments from Executives

"Most corporate cultures don't encourage the expression of new ideas, new perspectives. Good thinkers are often perceived as weird and don't make it up the ladder. Typically there is no motivation to learn, no recognition. People only get rewarded for short-term accomplishment, which is very different from learning."

"CEOs often tend to replicate themselves, which creates a past-looking environment. Organizations don't encourage learning unless there is a sense of urgency, a crisis. Equilibrium discourages learning. Also learning is an equilibrium-busting process and most corporations have a big investment in equilibrium."

"Learning per se isn't challenge; humans are always learning. What executives aren't doing is relearning or unlearning."

"Active learning that goes beyond the organization, industry, and even country is becoming important. In the past the organization trained managers with opportunities and courses. But the skills and perspectives now needed require the individual to experience an obligation to learn, to invest in a widely dispersed information network so he or she can tap into people with diverse knowledge. The effective executive has to see a complex world everyday, and this is a world of politics, technology, and economics."

"So much of what is interpreted these days as good or innovative leadership is simply attribution. When Mr. or Ms. X was here good things happened; therefore I attribute to them—that is, their skills and knowledge—the good things that occurred."

"Usually an executive doesn't know what has made the organization successful in the past. Not being sure, he or she holds tightly to a number of things related to the past, afraid to mess with them and unsure about why or how the organization became successful."

"There is difficulty with being broad and focused at the same time, balancing breadth of information with technical depth. Especially in this computer-generated information era, how can managers interpret the stories the numbers tell, see the broad picture in which the technical and logistical specifics are embedded? How can managers learn to use their intuition, in addition to the data, and deal with feelings and facts?"

"Executives must learn to live on the membrane—that is, they must acknowledge and respect organizational norms at the same time they are injecting uncomfortable challenges to the norms. They must also be able to enlist the support of a network—say five percent of the influentials in the organization—who will be able to get the support of another twenty percent.

This support may provide the credibility required to get a hearing for 'revolutionary' new ideas."

"The corporate environment as a teacher is more powerful than the individual's capacity to be a learner. But real leaders are ones who can transform ideas into action and who create and encourage learning opportunities, creating an environment in which people learn together."

"Leaders are generally smart enough to handle the complex; the unusual skill is the ability to take the complex (new learning) and make it simple in explaining or teaching it to others. Simplifying and selling are important aspects of leadership. One caution: simplification does not mean glibness. Thus the leader must truly understand the full complexity, as opposed to sound bytes or clever phrases."

"Executives often cut off learning by their give-it-to-me-in-five-minutes-or-in-a-one-page-executive-summary approach."

"New ideas coming from the outside, such as total quality management, often because they have a special label or packaging, become the responsibility of some special group who gets made accountable for them. The typical manager then doesn't have to think very deeply about what this new idea or concept means for his or her work and jobs."

"Much learning should come not from outside but from inside the organization, which means executives must have the ability to learn from their people. This requires the executive to establish an environment in which the truth can come out, in which it is safe to tell the truth."

"Top management doesn't get the time to go hunting outdoors, so they get used to shooting messengers who bring bad news. In my experience, news is so managed by the time it gets to the top of the organization that no one knows what is reality any more. No one will ever say anything like, 'You know we have a disaster on our hands in the X division.'"

"Also, these days people can be risk-averse, which accentuates the tendency for bad news to stay bottled up and therefore for senior management not to learn."

"In our corporation we are failing to think through new paradigms about how products or services can be produced or the nature of our markets."

"We only know how to be comfortable with what has been proven; we are not allowed to admit we're amateurs, just beginning."

"To be effective, an executive now has to be prepared to see a new world everyday, a world of politics and economics and technology as well as competition."

"Good executives, as learners, have a natural curiosity, are active, not passive, learners. It is often discernible by noting whether the person has varied interests, seeks broad exposures, doesn't restrict himself or herself to a narrow definition of their field of interest. Such a person is also often playful, even humorous. 'Anti-learners' are obsessed with always getting the right solution; they feign competency when thrown into a new area or into a problem set that is new for them. They are stingy with their effort; they meter it."

"Good learners are usually ones who can accept dissonance and ambiguity."

"It is worth exploring how executives can become more playful with ideas because people are often very creative when at play. Unfortunately corporations discourage playfulness."

"Where executives are in a learning mode, you can often feel the degree to which there is the sense of being on a roll, of really cooking, of getting it all together. Some executives are just very good at creating this spirit and setting up situations so that their subordinates will gain this sensation of being totally involved, open with one another, and creative. The good leader is one who almost radiates this joy of learning and can establish this kind of learning field."

"You have to invest in building what I call *information networks*, which can help you learn what is going on outside your own sphere and assist you in problem solving."

"The typical U.S. manager is just not patient enough to undertake the investigations necessary to learn new things—for instance, talking to a lot of those who are knowledgeable. Instead he or she wants immediate answers."

"We can hire good people because we encourage personal growth. We encourage curiosity. People can get involved in things they have an interest in even though they may not have the appropriate technical background. And we believe in a free flow of ideas so that at our meetings you won't be able to tell who has the more senior positions. We are always telling people that they are living in a world of continuous crises. In such a world you have to learn new things, innovate constantly, and do everything faster."

"In my experience the good managers know their strengths and weaknesses and seek to get themselves into situations which play to their strengths and avoid the others. For example, one successful executive I know is solely a deal-maker. So whenever he gets shifted he is quick to find good implementers, 'follow-uppers.' He makes things happen but can't go further. Another successful manager is superb at delegation and his people love him because they do all the stuff he can't do or doesn't like. He gets people to really throw themselves into these assignments through his ability to find their hot buttons. Whatever it takes to get you to sign on, he gives. It is only the third kind of executive who is a learner. The one I am thinking of purposely takes on assignments which are scary, really discomforting. Each time that person finishes one of these, he or she will say, 'I really learned something this time.'"

The Impact of U.S. Culture on U.S. Management

To what extent are the difficulties of adapting to new leadership styles the result of cultural values, not personal learning or personality? Managers are obviously products of their own cultures. In many ways, U.S. culture shaped and fostered the management style that was a very visible part of the enormous success of U.S. business during most of the twentieth century.

Perhaps the culture that was so consistent with the needs of an earlier style of production—particularly mechanistic, rigid mass production—is now an impediment to learning some of the new leadership styles required by fast-changing technologies and a more service-oriented economy.[6]

I have selected a few elements that I think are basic to U.S. culture: individualism and competitiveness; linearity, compartmentalization, and rational thinking; quantification and clarity; universalism; impatience; and pragmatic, not conceptual. I will discuss how each of these may relate to the leadership challenges discussed above.

Individualism and Competitiveness

The U.S. culture emphasizes individualism. People in the United States are used to viewing peers as competitors and tend to believe that they are in a winner-take-all race for individual success—whether in winning a high salary or profits or gaining recognition with a prestigious title. These values are responsible for our strong-willed entrepreneurs who succeed against great odds, as well as the spirited, even acrimonious, but often productive debates that take place at management meetings.

But such values can also inhibit useful cooperation and encourage destructive competition among peers in which a personal win becomes more important than success for the larger organization. Highly individualistic managers may struggle for as much autonomy and personal turf as possible and, in the process, detract from valuable interdependencies.

Yet U.S. individualism, in a world of fast-changing technologies and markets, can be functional, even critical. As organizations become more interdependent and work systems more complex, the so-called tight coupling among the components of work systems creates difficult integration problems. A good deal of individual initiative and personal responsibility is necessary to get the divergent, and sometimes incompatible, parts of the system to fit together. Perhaps only strong individuals will be willing to tell superiors bad news and disagree with high-level decisions that contradict the realities that are apparent at lower levels.

Organizations like Minnesota Mining have demonstrated also that entrepreneurial middle managers can create new businesses and new strategies even within large organizations. Why, then, do so few large companies appear to have senior managers who encourage the expression of counterintuitive, even countercultural, ideas and reward individuals who come up with ingenious answers to intractable problems and take personal risks to prove out their ideas?

Linearity, Compartmentalization, and Rational Thinking

U.S. executives have learned their organizational logic from a larger political philosophy and pragmatism that is based on an optimistic, reasonably predictable future. Throughout U.S. life, there is an emphasis on planfulness and the formalization of plans in precise, written form. There is the expectation that there will be a neat, linear, one-way progression from plans to implementation to results. And, in the past, careful planning could assume that the external technological and competitive system would remain reasonably stable.

The U.S. culture encouraged a segmented view of management and functions. Plans clearly came before execution, and execution was expected to move sequentially—for example, from planning, to development, to operations, to marketing. Clear separation of functions was good, just as was the clear separation of powers in our government. Yet realistically we know that most plans require continuous change; replanning or real-time planning is becoming important with the rapid changes occurring in markets and technology.

A world filled with chaotic change may make some of these cultural-managerial values less functional. Keynes is quoted as saying, "The inevitable never happens. It is the unexpected always." As the cliché has it, change is everywhere and the future is almost never predictable from the past. Most plans are dated before the ink is dry. Projects are devised on the run or even rationalized after execution. Unanticipated and unanticipatable events require improvisation and spontaneity. Perhaps the best strategy is the emergent one.

The boundaries between functions blur, and it can be a serious error to precisely demarcate jurisdictions. Most arguments over whether a critical decision is solely a marketing one or solely one for customer services are wastefully academic, because fast-paced internal coordination is needed to develop a new product or meet a competitor's price or specification, and usually there is continuous overlapping among functions.

The elaboration of staff, with increasing numbers and varieties of experts, not only works against the concept of a lean organization but, as we have seen, also complicates the everyday challenge for managers to achieve operating excellence, and it inhibits their learning of new and diverse technical ideas and concepts. The belief and often the senior-management practice of creating a separate new staff specialty for every new problem enormously complicates organizational processes.

Years ago a European executive told me how amused he was that the U.S. corporation he was dealing with had two separate departments to handle greeting foreign visitors. One was for those using air transportation and the other handled visitors who came by ship. I see no evidence that the temptation to specialize has abated.

Quantification and Clarity

In a culture that places great stress on written documents and precise, quantitative standards, it is not surprising that managers have grown used to unambiguous guidelines for action, expecting that there will be, or at least should be, clear wins and losses. Too many managers repeat the mantra: "It's only the bottom line that counts." Consistently, hard numbers drive out other criteria.

U.S. managers tend to grow edgy with ambiguity, with true contradictions and inconsistencies, and with situations where there aren't clear signposts and a clear scorecard. (That is why they find intolerable the absence of performance appraisals in many Asian organizations.) They assume that if something can't be given a quantitative measurement, it doesn't exist. Thus, subjective, intuitive, and qualitative factors often get short shrift.

Yet many critical issues in modern business can't be precisely quantified. Ambiguities and inconsistencies predominate, and cultures like those of the Far East—which for centuries have emphasized living with ambiguity—gain a competitive edge from their comfort with an absence of clarity and emphasis on fluidity and flexibility.

Universalism

People in the U.S. have been taught to seek out the *one* best way of doing things, the big answer, whether from consultants, management gurus or professors, or from surveys of best practice. Managers often assume that these "best ways" can just be implanted in all parts of a business with top-down fiat.

This faith in universal answers results in impatience with the need to build from the bottom up, to identify and work with what is unique about each situation. It is hardly surprising that there is widespread cynicism at lower levels about the current management fad. For example, many corporations go through predictable cycles of "We have to centralize" and then "We have to decentralize"—failing to recognize that perhaps both alternatives are simultaneously necessary and that there may not be one best solution.

Impatience

The U.S. propensity for recognizing that time is money and feeling driven by time has been functional, because coordination depends upon interlocking through time. But when working overseas, courting potential new-venture partners or customers, or even dealing with most human resources problems, the counting of every minute by typical U.S. managers can be quite destructive. Brought up to believe they must account for each minute, they experience great pressure when there aren't countable results equivalent to the time expended.

Pragmatic, Not Conceptual

Managers in the U.S. pride themselves on being pragmatic, having no theory, wanting just the facts, and using a one-page executive summary. At the extreme, this leads to an unwillingness to understand why and how things really work. Some of the endless reinventing of the wheel that occurs in the purchase of a new fad, and layering it on as the newest management program to solve our problems, results from this failure to look beneath the surface.

Comments from Executives

"From the first day we enter the educational system in the U.S. we are taught that it is important to succeed as an individual; team endeavors are not encouraged. We've grown up to think that learning is an individual endeavor and one is penalized for trying to learn together."

"I don't think most executives realize how ill-prepared we are as a nation to deal with multinational business issues. We are eccentric and arrogant, more than any other people I have encountered. We don't understand how frail our models are for doing business elsewhere in the world. Too many executives believe that one solution fits all, and something that has brought them great success will work anywhere."

"We don't realize how homogeneous we are compared to the rest of the world. We don't realize what an incredible thing it is to be able to travel 3,000 miles and find people who speak the same language, eat pretty much the same kinds of foods, and dress the same way."

Some Concluding Observations

What was unique about the conference was its foreswearing of magic bullets. Both the basic design and the quality of participants discouraged the search for simple solutions or models.

Rather than jumping to answers, the participants were willing to focus on problems. There was an unchallenged consensus that companies both contain and must react to a very turbulent world and that the old rules may not apply. The managerial world, all agreed, has become a very difficult place to do well and do it consistently.

Although no one opted for a version of the *great man theory*, there was very real agreement on the increasing importance of leadership. Leadership skills become ever more critical in a world of very great centrifugal forces and the market's (for goods and company shares) small tolerance for error.

Most scholars of leadership look askance at what has been called the great man theory—for reasons aside from its inherent sexism. There is general agreement that leadership is a process involving relationships among leaders and followers—and we could add involving "internal" peers and "external" peers (customers, vendors, partners, contractors).

Moving to a process view also requires us to consider the context in which leadership is exercised. The context has shifted dramatically in U.S. business from what we labeled, a bit disparagingly, *the comfort years*, to the extraordinarily pressureful world of global competition and an ever-accelerating pace of technological change.

Not too many years ago, leadership researchers "discovered" that R&D-type organizations, filled with unpredictability, required a very different style of management than routine production. In some sense, many of what used to be considered routine businesses have now become much more like R&D laboratories as products and services and work methods and even the market-place are in constant flux.

The demands on managers for high performance in a world of lean organizations, constant change, and incredible competitive pressures appear to conflict with the attitudes of many younger employees seeking a well-balanced life and even less responsibility.

Also troublesome are the body blows to company loyalty coming from repeated downsizings and the tenuous commitment of many companies to long-term employment relationships.

An important counterbalance can be a new superior-subordinate rela-tionship stemming from changes in markets and technology. In earlier de-cades, highly routinized, unchanging work and high levels of fixed assets often pitted workers against managers. And the gulf created was almost unbridgeable. Profitability was derived almost solely from higher volumes of output, and employees were constantly pressed to work harder.

In many of today's organizations, profitability is derived from flexibil-ity and adaptability, and employees can make very real contributions to high performance using their heads as well as their hands. And middle managers now have real functions in creating excellence; companies can no longer afford to have them simply as conduits or linking pins between hierarchical levels.

We at the Center already have research suggesting that managers who continuously solve work problems and evolve better ways of doing things earn both loyalty and performance. These managers view performance excellence as stemming from a management-worker partnership in finding better ways of doing high-quality work, not from greater toil and sweat. Quality and service and production problems, in these contexts, are viewed as challenges to managerial ingenuity and not, as in traditional companies, as a reflection of worker indolence.

In the "comfort years," many managers lost their claim to leadership by being on automatic pilot much of the time. Much of management was prac-ticed as a highly routine activity in which a few sound principles and reason-able personal skills were all that was needed. Unlike other professionals, managers did not keep learning, particularly if they had some early job successes.

Today, leadership and learning have come much closer together. That turbulence in markets and technology and the need to work with a wide variety of lateral internal and external peers means that the manager has to seek to understand the goals, values, and work methods of many organizations in addition to his or her own. Learning a foreign—that is, an overseas—culture is just an example of the need to comprehend multiple organizational cultures as the emphasis on seamless systems of work flow take the place of the neat compartments and secure boundaries separating functions and organizations. Every manager now needs to be a systems manager.

Executive teams are a good example of the need for adaptability and learning. They are often made up of managers who share little in the way of common experience or even common short-run goals.

More and more decisions involve contradictions and almost equally opposed forces (or inducements). Thus leaders who are used to a simple calculus or well-honed, formula answers are likely to fail. The performance demands are just too high for a leader who isn't adaptive and isn't learning to succeed over a period of time. To be sure, the use of threats or the ability to make severe cuts (in products, facilities, and people) may enable a poor but tough leader to look good in the short run. But over time, the complex footwork required to penetrate new markets and master new technologies will trip up executives whose major skill is pushing things through.

As many have noted, these "new" leaders' days are filled with ambiguity and inconsistency. Senior executives are asked to exercise strategic judgment to produce long-run organizational returns. At the same time they must meet very short-term demands of the unforgiving stock market. Leadership is inevitably associated with both vision and perseverance, and yet increasing uncertainty and rapid changes in technology and the boundaries of markets make it more and more difficult to demonstrate these qualities.

Today's leaders also have new temptations. As more executives appear to act like owners—that is, in some well-publicized cases they receive income levels we used to associate with the founders and owners of a business when they sold their holdings—surely many must be tempted to seek media-star earnings. There are comparable temptations to violate ethical standards in order to meet the ceaseless demands for improved quarterly earnings. Those who succumb probably forfeit any chance of being respected for their leadership by their organizations.

At the conference, I gave my view of leadership: "The leader integrates the threats and opportunities from outside and facilitates the adaptation and response of his or her systems and personnel into a coherent strategy."

Much to the reassurance of the conference planners, the participants endorsed the themes or problem areas we had identified in our pre-conference research. Although, as noted above, there were no ringing answers pronounced, there was surprising unanimity around the identification of what was most challenging to contemporary managers.

To most of us it appears as though the leadership field must move profoundly to reflect the enormous changes in the context in which leadership is practiced. Just a few years ago most students of the field were concentrating on the leader's proper balance between work and people interests. How very far we have come since then!

Bibliography

Bok, D. (1994). *The cost of talent: How executives and professionals are paid and how it affects America*. New York: The Free Press.

Bounds, W. (1994, March 29). Kodak to ask computer firms for alliances. *The Wall Street Journal*, p. A3.

Brandt, J. R. (1994, May 2). Middle management: Where the action will be. *Industry Week*, pp. 30–36.

Bunker, K. A., & Webb, A. D. (1992). *Learning how to learn from experience: Impact of stress and coping* (Report No. 154). Greensboro, NC: Center for Creative Leadership.

Burgelman, R. A. (1983). A process model of internal corporate venturing. *Administrative Science Quarterly*, pp. 223–244.

Burgelman, R. A., & Sayles, L. R. (1986). *Inside corporate innovation: Strategy, structure, and managerial skills*. New York: The Free Press.

Burnside, R. M., & Guthrie, V. A. (1992). *Training for action: A new approach to executive development* (Report No. 153). Greensboro, NC: Center for Creative Leadership.

Byrne, J., Brandt, R., & Port, O. (1993, February 8). The virtual corporation. *Business Week*, pp. 98–102.

Carroll, P. (1994). *Big blues*. New York: Morrow.

Chernow, R. (1994, April 1). Ferocious competition. *The Wall Street Journal*, p. A8.

Cox, J. (1994, May 23). Two firms' views on human rights. *USA Today*, p. B3.

De Meuse, K. P., & Tornow, W. W. (1993). Leadership and the changing psychological contract between employer and employee. *Issues & Observations, 13*(2), 4–6.

Deutchman, A. (1994, May 2). How H-P continues to grow and grow. *Fortune, 129*(9), 90.

Galbraith, J. K. (1967). *The new industrial state*. Boston: Houghton Mifflin.

Handy, C. (1992, November-December). Balancing corporate power. *Harvard Business Review*, pp. 59–72.

Hirschorn, L., & Gilmore, T. (1992, May-June). The boundaries of the boundaryless company. *Harvard Business Review*, pp. 104–115.

Hwang, S. L. (1994, April 4). Ding-dong: Updating Avon means respecting history without repeating it. *The Wall Street Journal*, p. A1.

Ingrassia, P., & Mitchell, J. (1994, March 31). Ford to realign with a system of global chiefs. *The Wall Street Journal*, p. A3.

Johnson, K. (1994, April 3). Workers become job hunters as company reinvents itself. *The New York Times*, Sec. 1, p. 19.

Katzenbach, J. R., & Smith, D. K. (1993). *The wisdom of teams: Creating the high-performance organization*. Boston: Harvard Business School Press.

Kegan, R. (1982). *The evolving self: Problem and process in human development.* Cambridge, MA: Harvard University Press.

Kelley, R. (1988, November-December). In praise of followers. *Harvard Business Review*, pp. 142–148.

Likert, R. (1961). *New patterns of management.* New York: McGraw-Hill.

McCarthy, M. J. (1994, March 31). USAir names finance officer to be president. *The Wall Street Journal*, p. B5.

Miller, D. (1990). *The Icarus paradox.* New York: Harper Business.

Mintzberg, H. (1987, July-August). Crafting strategy. *Harvard Business Review*, pp. 66–75.

Noer, D. (1993a). *Healing the wounds: Overcoming the trauma of layoffs and revitalizing downsized organizations.* San Francisco: Jossey-Bass.

Noer, D. (1993b). Leadership in an age of layoffs. *Issues & Observations, 13*(3), 1–6.

Pascale, R. (1990). *Managing on the edge: How the smartest companies use conflict to stay ahead.* New York: Simon and Schuster.

Peace, W. (1991, November-December). The hard work of being a soft manager. *Harvard Business Review*, pp. 40–42, 46–47.

Salwen, K. G. (1994, March 16). White House puts stress on skills for job security. *The Wall Street Journal*, p. A2.

Sayles, L. (1990). *Redefining what's essential to business performance: Pathways to productivity, quality, and service* (Report No. 142). Greensboro, NC: Center for Creative Leadership.

Sayles, L. (1993). *The working leader: The triumph of high performance over conventional management principles.* New York: The Free Press.

Simison, R. L., Lavin, D., & Mitchell, J. (1994, May 4). Tooling along: With auto profits up, big three again get a major opportunity. *The Wall Street Journal*, p. A1.

Vaill, P. (1989). *Managing as a performing art.* San Francisco: Jossey-Bass.

Notes

1. I believe that a good share of our leadership principles or prescriptions of good practice are derived from two sources. Some are what could be called *generic* or *historical*. They represent universal verities about the skills and behavior associated with leaders who "make a difference" and who gain high levels of commitment from their followers.

Other leadership prescriptions are model-driven. They grow out of theories about leadership that may have been derived from empirical research. A good example is the classical leadership model that prescribes a balance between work-oriented and people-oriented behaviors.

There has been less attention to contextual-based leadership knowledge—that is, to leadership skills that are situationally specific. In seeking to look at correlates of organizational and environmental turbulence, we are moving into this third area.

2. A popular treatment of the management of teams is the work of Jon Katzenbach and Douglas Smith (1993, pp. 111–120).

3. In assessing the impact of corporate downsizing, it may be useful to remember that the view that work and career limited to a single organization was a benefit enjoyed only by that segment of the workforce employed by certain larger, more stable organizations. In a recent international conference on jobs and job security, President Clinton observed that the average American worker will change employers seven or eight times in his or her work life (Salwen, 1994).

4. For a recent overview of executive salaries in relation to the compensation of other groups in American society, see Derek Bok (1994).

5. A major aspect of this shift is a refocusing on the customer. Almost all companies are reorganizing to emphasize quick response to, and satisfaction of, their customers.

6. It is possible that Japan's recent success has had more to do with its underlying culture than with its specific management techniques.

www.ingramcontent.com/pod-product-compliance
Lightning Source LLC
Chambersburg PA
CBHW080721220326
41520CB00056B/7360